Play and Discover
PLANTS

Caryn Jenner

W

FRANKLIN WATTS

LONDON · SYDNEY

First published in 2014
by Franklin Watts

Copyright © Franklin Watts 2014

Franklin Watts
338 Euston Road
London NW1 3BH

Franklin Watts Australia
Level 17/207 Kent Street
Sydney, NSW 2000

Series editor: Sarah Peutrill
Design: Basement68

Dewey number: 580
HB ISBN: 978 1 4451 3139 9
Library ebook ISBN: 978 1 4451 3140 5

Printed in China

Franklin Watts is a division
of Hachette Children's Books,
an Hachette UK company.

www.hachette.co.uk

Picture credits: Absoluteindia/Dreamstime: 7tr. Alexmak72427/Dreamstime: 22t. Steve Allen/ Dreamstime: 13 inset. Noam Armonn/Shutterstock: front cover l. Christian Baitg/istockphoto: 6, 23cb. Darren Baker/Shutterstock: 2br, 9l. Harald Biebel/ Dreamstime: 14cl, 23c. Alexandr Blinov /Dreamstime: 18b, 23clb, 24t. Buketgvozdey/Dreamstime: 7tl. George Burba/Dreamstime: 8br. Lian Deng/Dreamstime: 20. Mikhail Dudarev / Shutterstock: 23tcl. egluteskarota/Shutterstock: 19b. Evgenyi44/Dreamstime: 17tl, 17bcb. George Filyagin/ Shutterstock: 22b. Joe Gough/istockphoto: 18c. Gryzeva/Dreamstime: 17ba. hektor2/istockphoto: 21b. Jarihin/Dreamstime: 8bc. kingjon/istockphoto: 17cr, 17bc. Kolotype /Dreamstime: 16, 17bt. Iurii Konoval/ Dreamstime: 14l. val lawless/Shutterstock: 3b, 19t. Filip Lenkiewicz/Dreamstime: 4t. Leopollo/Dreamstime: 5b, 23clc. Majaan/Dreamstime: 17cl. Monkey Business Images/ Dreamstime: 13br. Mrdomsx/Dreamstime: 11c. Denis Nata/Shutterstock: 8tc, 23crb, 23bl. Kotomiti Okuma/ Dreamstime: 1, 9r. Qpicimages/Dreamstime: 19 main. Paul Paladin/ istockphoto: 14c, 14b. Photogenes: 2tl, 13bg, 23tcr, 23br. Photos1st/Dreamstime: 8tl. Valentina Razumova/ Shutterstock: 10, 23cl, 23cr, 23clcb, 23bcl. Goce Risteski/ Dreamstime: 4b. Elena Schweitzer/Shutterstock: front cover r. Dimitri Surkov/Dreamstime: 21t, 23tr. tiler84/ istockphoto: 15l. Uptail/Dreamstime: 5t, 23bc. windujedi/ istockphoto: 17c, 17b. Wrangel/istockphoto: 14cr. XiXinXing/Shutterstock: 15r. Hongqi Zhang (aka Michael Zhang)/Dreamstime: 11t.

Every attempt has been made to clear copyright. Should there be any inadvertent omission please apply to the publisher for rectification.

Contents

What are plants?

Trees ➡ are plants.
Flowers ➡ are plants.

These strawberries are plants too.

Even grass is a plant.

Planting

I plant
a seed
in the soil.

A plant needs water and light.

Then it grows and grows and grows!

Growing

We're pretending to be plants.

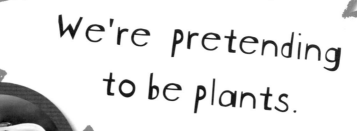

I'm a small seedling, starting to grow.

I'm growing and growing. I've got leaves now.

8

Look at me! I'm tall with a great big flower. What am I?

I'm a sunflower.

9

Flowers

← A flower has petals, a stem and leaves...

and roots that ← grow under the ground.

Trees

I paint a tall tree trunk.

The branches are the fingers on my handprint.

Then I paint lots and lots of green leaves on the branches.

13

Leaves

Willow

These leaves come from different trees.

Horse chestnut

Oak

Holly

Birch

Look, they have different shapes.

14

My plant picture

We're collecting leaves for a plant picture.

16

Twig

Conker

Pine cone

Acorn

These things also come from plants.

We stick them all down to make a plant picture.

17

Food from plants

Lots of food comes from plants, like this potato.

Potatoes grow in the ground.

19

Plants everywhere

We're on a treasure hunt to find plants.

I found some bright red flowers.

21

Draw a giant garden

Make a giant garden picture with your friends. Ask everyone to draw lots of green trees, colourful flowers and other plants. How about drawing some fruits and vegetables too? You can use crayons, paints, felt-tip pens or coloured pencils. Cut out all of your plant pictures. Then take turns sticking the plant pictures onto a giant sheet of paper using glue or sticky tape. The more plants you draw, the bigger your garden will be! Ask permission to stick the plant picture on a wall.

Word bank

apple

branches

dandelion

flower

grass

leaf

petals

potatoes

roots

seed

seedling

soil

stem

strawberries

trees

Index

Notes for parents and teachers

Planting – Children love growing their own plants. You'll need seeds, such as watercress, beans, or flowers, plant pots and soil. Help the children fill the pots with soil, make a small hole for the seeds and cover with more soil. Water the plants and place them in a sunny spot. Observe the plants over time and share the children's excitement as they grow!

Growing – Use role play to show children how plants grow. A sunflower is a good example. First, have the children curl up small like a sunflower seed. Then, slowly, they start growing taller and taller and developing leaves. Finally, the flower opens and stretches tall to face the sun.

Flowers – Help children learn basic parts of flowers. Prepare flower parts in advance using coloured paper to make: soil with roots; stem with leaves; different types of petals. Discuss how to put these parts together to make a finished flower. Then let the children stick the parts down to make their own flower.

Trees – Children will have fun using handprints to paint trees. First, paint the tree trunk. At the top, make a handprint, spreading their fingers to make tree branches. Then paint leaves on the branches. How about adding some blossom to the tree, or perhaps apples or oranges?

Leaves – Encourage children to use observation skills to look at different kinds of leaves. They could use a magnifying glass for an even closer look. Discuss how leaves have different shapes and come from different kinds of tree. Ask the children to describe the leaves and sort them.

Plant picture – Take the children outside to collect things that come from plants, such as leaves, twigs, acorns, conkers, bits of bark, flower petals, etc. Make sure they only collect things on the ground and not from a growing plant. Use glue to stick these plant treasures onto card to make a collage.

Food from plants – Children will enjoy making potato stamp pictures. To prepare, cut potatoes into large pieces. If desired, carve a simple design into the cut end. Have the children brush paint onto the cut end of the potato and stamp it onto paper or card to make a picture. You can also use apples, carrots or parsnips.

Plants everywhere – Take the children on a plant treasure hunt to find all sorts of plants in your local area. Encourage the children to examine the plants and describe them. See if the children can even identify some plants. Just beware of nettles and other spiky and poisonous plants!